Nutrition recommendations during TCM - Stomach - Rebellious Qi

Please check these recommendations always with a nutrition consultant, therapist, doctor or dietician. The recipes and the list of ingredients are supporting the conventional medical therapy. The calorie disclosures of fresh ingredients (fruit and vegetables) vary according to quality and time of harvest. The contents were checked by a dietician and a nutrition consultant for the Traditional Chinese Medicine (TCM).

Author:
©2020 Josef Miligui
www.ebns.at

Source:
The lists are created from the EBNS database for nutritional counseling. The database is used by dietitians, therapists and doctors for advising the patient / client.

Literature:
The specialist literature and the training documents of the German and Austrian dietary and traditional Chinese medicine serve as a knowledge base. We have used the documents as a basis of knowledge, adapted it to our experience and completed them.
http://nutribook.info/

Production and publishing:
BoD – Books on Demand, Norderstedt
ISBN: 9783752894035

Nutrition recommendations for TCM - Stomach - Rebellious Qi

1 Treatment strategy

Lower the stomach Qi, harmonize and strengthen the stomach.

2 Avoid

Eating too fast, eating too much, chewing badly, getting excited, arguing, big meals with many ingredients, indigestible food, late meal, too spicy food.

3 Breakfast

4 Snack

5 Lunch

6   Afternoon

7   Dinner

8   Any time

9 Recipes

(rec.) = You can use more.
(little) = You should use less than specified
(omit) = omit.

9.1 Apple sauce with raisins

Nourishes fluids, reduces stomach heat, strengthens spleen, harmonizes stomach, moisturizes, relaxes, builds up Qi.
Cooking time approx. 25 min
Calories p. portion: 74
10 portions
Allergens: O

Quantity of ingredients

Apple (sweet) 2,2 lbs / 1000g. (little) - cool - sweet, sour ....earth
Water 1/2 cup / 100g. (yes) - cool - salty.. ....earth
Raisins 1/8 lbs - 2oz / 50g. (little) - warm – sweet.......................................earth

Cooking instructions:

Wash, peel and quarter the apples and remove the core. Put the apples with the water in a pot. Wash the raisins with hot water and add them. Cook at low heat for about 10 minutes, then allow to cool. For children up to 10 months, mash in the blender finely. For the larger ones, crush with the potato steamer. Fill and seal n a freezer or empty yoghurt jug. Close the yoghurt jug. Freeze in the shock freezer.
If necessary, thaw at room temperature for about 6 hours. (Lasting about 4 months).
The fruit mousse is intended as dessert or intermediate meal. It has an anti-digestive effect. In case of diarrhea give better banana.

9.2 Barley mash with berries

Forces essence, forces spleen, cools bladder, diuretic, relaxes, builds up Qi, spreads, moisturises dryness.
Cooking time approx. 2 hours
Calories p. portion: 113
5 portions
Allergens: A

Quantity of ingredients

Water 10 cups / 1200g. (yes) - cool - salty ....earth
Barley 1 cup / 120g. (little) - cool - sweet, little salty...................................earth
Ginger fresh 2 slices / 2g. (rec.) - warm - acrid ....metal
Cardamom 3 capsules / 1g. () - warm - acrid .... *
Salt 1 pinch / 1g. (little) - cold - salty ....water
Raspberry 5/8 lbs - 8oz / 250g. () - neutral - sweet, sour ....wood
Cocoa 1 pinch / 1g. (little) - warm - sweet, bitter ....fire
Barley malt 1 table spoon / 15g. () - cool - sweet ....earth
Lemon Balm (fresh) 2-4 leaves / 3g. () - cool - sour ....metal

Cooking instructions:

Boil the barley with water, ginger and cardamom pods in a large saucepan. Close pot with a lid and cook over low heat for about 2 hours.

For 2 servings of cooked barley porridge, place about 2 ladles in a bowl. Stir with sunflower seeds, malt, cocoa powder and a pinch of salt. Stir fresh berries into the porridge and serve sprinkled with fresh mint or lemon balm.

Tip: The pre-cooked barley porridge (without fruit) can be stored well in the refrigerator and used for sweet or savory dishes, e.g. with stewed vegetables or fruit seasoned compote.

9.3   Barley soup

Works neutral to slightly warming and relaxes the Qi flow. Helps with loss of appetite and diarrhea due to spleen weakness. With weak spleen qi, one should often eat salty soups for breakfast.
Cooking time approx. 25 min
Calories p. portion: 265
2 portions
Allergens: A

Quantity of ingredients

Barley 1 cup / 120g. (little) - cool - sweet, little salty...................................earth
Salt 1 pinch / 1g. (little) - cold - salty ....water
Ginger fresh 1/2 teaspoon / 1g. (rec.) - warm - acrid...............................metal
Olive oil 1 table spoon / 10g. (little) - cool - sweet ....earth
Parsley 3 table spoons / 30g. (yes) - warm - bitter ....wood
Water 1 1/2 cups / 240g. (yes) - cool - salty ....earth

Cooking instructions:

Roast the barley in the pan, then grind it to the ground, and boil with water, some salt and ginger to a mash. Before serving add oil and parsley.

Variant: You can add a better taste to the dish if you cook it with prepared vegetable or meat broth.

9.4 Basic recipe for a beef broth (clear)

Strengthens Qi and Yang, is very warming.
Cooking time approx. 4-8 hours
Calories p. portion: 114
10 portions
Allergens: O

Quantity of ingredients

Beef soup meat 1,1 lbs / 500g. () - warm - sweet......................................earth
Beef meatbones 5/8 oz / 200g. () - warm - sweet....................................earth
Vinegar (Red wine vinegar) 1 dash / 3g. () - warm - sour, bitter............... wood
Juniper berry 8 pieces / 6g. (yes) - warm - sweet, acrid, bitter.....................fire
Rosemary 1 pinch / 1g. (yes) - warm - bitter.............. ....fire
Carrot 3 pieces / 210g. (rec.) - neutral - sweet...... ....earth
Parsnip 2 pieces / 300g. (rec.) - cool - bitter.......... ....fire
Leek 1 piece / 200g. (little) - warm - acrid.............. ....metal
Ginger fresh 1/2 teaspoon / 5g. (rec.) - warm - acrid...............................metal
Lovage 1 stem / 15g. (yes) - warm - acrid, bitter... ....metal
Lovage 1 stem / 15g. (yes) - warm - acrid, bitter... ....metal
Clove 2 pieces / 2g. (yes) - warm - acrid.............. ....metal
Pimento 6 pieces / 12g. () - hot - acrid ....metal
Anise (Common Fennel) 2 pieces / 1g. (rec.) - warm - acrid.....................earth
Salt 1 teaspoon / 5g. (little) - cold - salty ....water
Water 3,3 lbs / 1300g. (yes) - cool - salty.............. ....earth

Cooking instructions:

Heat water, a dash of red wine vinegar, some juniper berries, a little rosemary, bones and meat till it boils; add carrot, parsnip, leek, ginger, lovage, clove, allspice, star anise and a little salt; simmer for 4-8 hours then strain.
Refrigerate for later use.

9.5   Basic recipe for a chicken broth worming

Strengthens Qi and blood, is very warm.
Cooking time approx. 2-3 hours
Calories p. portion: 90
9 portions
Allergens: L

Quantity of ingredients
Chicken meat 1/2 piece / 600g. (little) - warm - sweet.............................. wood
Carrot 2 pieces / 150g. (rec.) - neutral - sweet..earth
Leek 1 stick / 45g. (little) - warm - acrid.. metal
Celery root 1 piece / 500g. (yes) - cool - sweet ....earth
Ginger fresh 2 slices / 2g. (rec.) - warm - acrid .... metal
Juniper berry 1 teaspoon / 3g. (yes) - warm - sweet, acrid, bitter.................fire
Bay leaf 3 pieces / 2g. () - warm - acrid.. *
Water 4 cup / 900g. (yes) - cool - salty...earth

Cooking instructions:
Remove chicken parts from fat. Place chicken pieces in a saucepan
with hot water and heat till it boils briefly, skimming any resulting foam.
Add coarsely chopped vegetables and all spices and cook over medium
heat for 2 to 3 hours. Strain the finished soup. Throw away vegetables
and bones.
Tip: If you want to use the meat as a soup insert, take out after 45
minutes and return only the bones in the soup.
Refrigerate for later use.

9.6   Basic recipe for a reissue soup (Congee)

Warms the stomach and spleen, harmonizes the intestine, forces Qi,
reduces moisture.
Cooking time approx. 2-4 hours
Calories p. portion: 140
3 portions

Quantity of ingredients
Rice variety any 1 cup / 120g. () - warm - sweet .... metal
Water 6 cups / 700g. (yes) - cool - salty ....earth

Cooking instructions:
Cook rice and water in a ratio of about 1: 6. The amount of water
determines the thickness of the mash (matter of taste).
Put the rice in a saucepan with a heavy lid. It is important to simmer the
rice after a short boil on the slightest flame, otherwise it burns.

Boil the rice for 2-4 hours. The longer he cocks, the more he strengthens.
If you want to eat the dish for breakfast, you can put the rice on just before bedtime.
To be on the safe side, you should first check the behavior of your pot and cooker under observation for a similar amount of time, so that nothing burns.
Refrigerate for later use.

9.7 Basic recipe for a vegetable soup, nutritious

Strengthens spleen and lung, regulates Qi flow, builds up Qi, dries out, passes downwardly, strengthens stomach Qi.
Cooking time approx. 2-3 hours
Calories p. portion: 48
5 portions
Allergens: L

Quantity of ingredients

Olive oil 1 table spoon / 4g. (little) - cool - sweet ....earth
Onion white 1 piece / 60g. (little) - warm - acrid ....metal
Carrot 3 pieces / 200g. (rec.) - neutral - sweet ....earth
Parsnip 3/8 lbs - 6oz / 150g. (rec.) - cool - bitter ....fire
Celery root 1 cup / 100g. (yes) - cool - sweet...earth
Ginger fresh 1/2 teaspoon / 2g. (rec.) - warm - acrid................................metal
Lemon 1/2 piece / 25g. () - cold - sour...wood
Juniper berry 6 pieces / 6g. (yes) - warm - sweet, acrid, bitter ....fire
Thyme dried 1 pinch / 1g. () - warm - bitter ....metal
Lovage 1 table spoon / 3g. (yes) - warm - acrid, bitter ....metal
Bay leaf 2 leaves / 1g. () - warm - acrid... *
Salt 1 pinch / 1g. (little) - cold - salty ....water
Water 3 cups / 650g. (yes) - cool - salty...earth

Cooking instructions:

Cut the vegetables into cubes.
Heat oil in hot pot, fry shortly onions and vegetables.
Add cold water, then add ginger, bay leaf and lemon juice.
Season with juniper, thyme and lovage. Cover for 2 - 3 hours on a low heat and simmer.
The used vegetables should be thrown away
The basic recipe serves as a soup base and to refine vegetables, legumes or cereals.
If you want to eat vegetable soup immediately, add the desired vegetables half an hour before.
Refrigerate for later use.

9.8   Blueberry puree

Keeps fluids and essence, forces liver and kidneys, forces blood, forces eyesight, warms spleen- and kidney-Yang, directs upwards, warms the stomach and spleen, promotes blood circulation and conduction flow, relieves cold-sickness and pain.
Cooking time approx. 10 min
Calories p. portion: 10
1 portions

Quantity of ingredients

Blueberry 1/2 oz / 20g. () - cool - sweet, sour.. wood
Cinnamon ground 1 pinch / 0,1g. (little) - hot - acrid, sweet .... *
Clove 1 piece / 1g. (yes) - warm - acrid.. metal
Water 1 cup / 250g. (yes) - cool - salty ....earth

Cooking instructions:

Boil blueberries with cinnamon and clove in water for 10 minutes. Remove the cinnamon and clove. Puree. Sweet as desired.

9.9   Carrot and rice gruel soup

Warms the stomach and spleen, harmonizes the intestine, forces Qi, reduces moisture, strengthens spleen and liver, regulates Qi flow, moisturizes, relaxes, builds up Qi, spreads.
Cooking time approx. 10 min
Calories p. portion: 101
1 portions

Quantity of ingredients

Basic recipe for a rice soup (Congee) 1 cup / 120g. (rec.) - neutral - sweet..... *
Carrot 2 pieces / 100g. (rec.) - neutral - sweet ....earth
Salt 1 teaspoon / 4g. (little) - cold - salty .... water

Cooking instructions:

Peel and grate carrots. Heat the rice soup (according to the basic recipe) till it boils and add the grated carrots and salt. Cook for 10 minutes.

9.10 Chicken soup with egg yolk and parsley

Forces Qi and blood, is very warming, nourishes blood and liver,
harmonizes liver and spleen, forces eyesight, preserves the fluids,
contracts.
Cooking time approx. 10 min
Calories p. portion: 118
2 portions
Allergens: CL

Quantity of ingredients

Basic recipe for a chicken soup (warming) 2 cup / 500g. () - warm - * .... *
Chicken yolk 1 piece / 10g. () - neutral - sweet ....earth
Parsley 1 table spoon / 10g. (yes) - warm - bitter......................................wood

Cooking instructions:

Cook the chicken broth according to the basic recipe.
Heat broth and bubble the egg yolk. Sprinkle the chopped parsley over
it and let it rest for about 2 minutes. Drink in small sips.

9.11 Compote from apples

Nourishes fluids, reduces stomach heat, forces spleen, produces
essence, harmonizes stomach, warms the stomach and spleen,
promotes blood circulation and conduction flow, relieves cold-sickness
and pain.
Cooking time approx. 10 min
Calories p. portion: 67
2 portions

Quantity of ingredients

Apple (sweet) 1 piece / 220g. (little) - cool - sweet, sour............................earth
Water 1 1/2 cups / 220g. (yes) - cool - salty...earth
Cinnamon ground 1 pinch / 1g. (little) - hot - acrid, sweet ....*

Cooking instructions:

Cook the apples (organic) with the skin and seeds. Sprinkle with
cinnamon.

9.12 Compote from plums

Warms the stomach and spleen, promotes blood circulation and conduction flow, relieves cold-sickness and pain.
Cooking time approx. 10 min
Calories p. portion: 22
2 portions

Quantity of ingredients
Plums 1/4 lbs - 4oz / 100g. () - warm - sweet, sour .... wood
Water 1 1/2 cups / 240g. (yes) - cool - salty ....earth
Cinnamon ground 1 pinch / 1g. (little) - hot - acrid, sweet .... *

Cooking instructions:
Boil plums in water until soft. Sprinkle with a little cinnamon.

9.13 Compote of local fruit and dried fruit

Moisturizes lungs, cools heat, reduces lung mucus, produces humors, relaxes, builds up Qi, spreads, nourishes fluids, reduces stomach heat, forces spleen, produces essence, harmonizes stomach, dries out, passes downwardly.
Cooking time approx. 15 min
Calories p. portion: 45
4 portions

Quantity of ingredients
Apple (sweet) 1 piece / 150g. (little) - cool - sweet, sour ....earth
Pear 1 piece / 150g. (little) - cool - sweet, sour ....earth
Cinnamon ground 1 pinch / 0,2g. (little) - hot - acrid, sweet .... *
Lemon peel 1/2 teaspoon / 2g. (little) - cool - bitter ....fire
Water 2 cup / 500g. (yes) - cool - salty..earth

Cooking instructions:
Cook the apple and pear with the dried fruit until soft. Sprinkle with cinnamon and lemon zest (organic).

9.14 Corn coffee with cardamom

Dries out, passes downwardly.
Cooking time approx. 5 min
Calories p. portion: 3
1 portions

Quantity of ingredients
Cereal coffee 1 table spoon / 15g. (little) - warm - bitter...............................fire
Cardamom 2 cores / 1g. () - warm - acrid.............. .... *
Water 1 cup / 120g. (yes) - cool - salty................. ....earth

Cooking instructions:
Boil water, coffee, sugar and cardamom. Let it set for one min before drinking.

9.15 Cottage cheese with steamed fruit

Moisturizes lungs, cools heat, reduces lung mucus, produces humors, moisturizes, relaxes, builds up Qi, spreads, preserves the fluids, contracts.
Cooking time approx. 20 min
Calories p. portion: 214
2 portions
Allergens: G

Quantity of ingredients
Cottage cheese 3/4 lbs / 300g. () - cool - sour .... wood
Apple (sour) 1 piece / 100g. (little) - cool - sour.. wood
Pear 1 piece / 100g. (little) - cool - sweet, sour ....earth

Cooking instructions:
Wash apples and pears well, do not peel, and chop small. In a pot with steam filter, boil them al dente, remove and allow to cool down.
Serve the cheese, spread the fruit on it.

9.16 Cranberry juice

Cools heart heat, nourishes heart blood and Yin.
Cooking time approx. 5 min
Calories p. portion: 43
1 portions

Quantity of ingredients
Cranberries 2 table spoons / 25g. () - cool - sour .... *
Water 1 cup / 125g. (yes) - cool - salty .... earth
Honey 1 table spoon / 10g. () - cold - sweet .... earth

Cooking instructions:
Mix the cranberries with a little water with the blender to a pulp. Add the remaining water and sweeten with the honey.

9.17 Grapefruit juice

Nourishes fluids, passes downwardly, forms body fluid.
Cooking time approx. 5 min
Calories p. portion: 107
1 portions

Quantity of ingredients
Grapefruit (Pomelo) 1 cup / 250g. (rec.) - cool - sweet, sour .... fire

Cooking instructions:
Juice fresh grapefruit or use organic juice.

9.18 Grated apple

Preserves the fluids, contracts.
Cooking time approx. 10 min
Calories p. portion: 120
1 portions

Quantity of ingredients
Apple (sour) 1 piece / 200g. (little) - cool - sour .... wood

Cooking instructions:
Peel apple and grate as fine as possible. Leave for at least 5 minutes until it turns brown.

9.19 Kohlrabi Potatoes mash

Moves Qi and blood, reduces moisture, forces Qi, forces spleen, relieves inflammation, moisturizes, relaxes, builds up Qi, spreads, forces kidney Jing.
Cooking time approx. 25 min
Calories p. portion: 278
1 portions
Allergens: CG

Quantity of ingredients
Kohlrabi 1/2 piece / 150g. (yes) - neutral - acrid, sweet ....earth
Potato 1/4 lbs - 4oz / 100g. (yes) - neutral - sweet...................................earth
Butter organic 1 table spoon / 10g. (yes) - neutral - sweet.........................earth
Chicken yolk 1 piece / 25g. () - neutral - sweet ....earth

Cooking instructions:
Remove the kohlrabi leaves, wash the tuber and tender leaves and the potatoes thoroughly. Peel the kohlrabi and potatoes, cut into cubes about 1 cm in size. Melt half the butter in a small saucepan, add the kohlrabi and the potatoes and fry in it. Steam with 2 tablespoons of water in a closed saucepan over low heat for about 15 minutes. Meanwhile, free the tenderest kohlrabi leaves from the stems and chop very finely. In total, at most 2 tablespoons of leaf pieces should be used. Add this to the vegetables about 5 minutes before the end of the cooking time. Stir in the egg yolk and bring to the boil again. Put the vegetables in a plate and mix with the remaining butter and egg yolk. (Crush for the baby with a fork.)

9.20 Miso soup with tofu

Nourish the humors, preserves the fluids, contracts, nourishes fluids, lets Qi ascend, harmonizes spleen and stomach, moisturizes, relaxes, builds up Qi, spreads, regulates Qi, warms spleen and kidney, dissolves stagnation, directs upwards.
Cooking time approx. 5 min
Calories p. portion: 51
3 portions
Allergens: E

Quantity of ingredients

Wakame 1 piece / 5g. () - cold - salty .... water
Miso 3-4 table spoons / 30g. (rec.) - neutral - salty .... water
Soy Tofu 1/8 lbs - 2oz / 50g. (rec.) - cool - sweet...................................... earth
Water 2 cup / 500g. (yes) - cool - salty... earth
Soy sauce 1 dash / 3g. () - cold - salty .... water
Onion (spring onion) 1/2 teaspoon / 6g. (little) - warm - acrid................... metal

Cooking instructions:

Boil soybean seedlings, wakame algae and diced tofu for 5 minutes.
Put the miso paste in the soup plate and slowly pour over the soup.
Season with Tamari sauce. Sprinkle with cutted spring onion.

9.21 Noodle casserole with plugs and peaches

Nourishes Yin and Jing of heart and kidney, reduces internal heat,
preserves the fluids, contracts, moisturizes, calms nerves and stomach,
strengthens blood and fluids, brings blood into motion, builds up Qi,
spreads, warms the stomach and spleen.
Cooking time approx. 1 hour
Calories p. portion: 442
4 portions
Allergens: ACGO

Quantity of ingredients

Peaches 1,1 lbs / 500g. (yes) - warm - sour, sweet .... earth
Noodles (wheat, ribbon noodles) with egg 5/8 oz / 200g. () - cool - sweet, salty
   wood
Chicken egg 2 pieces / 120g. (yes) - neutral - sweet .... earth
Sugar - icing sugar 1/8 lbs - 2oz / 40g. () - cold - sweet .... earth
Vanilla sugar natural 3 package / 3g. () - neutral - sweet .... *
Lemon peel 1/2 piece / 2g. (little) - cool - bitter .... fire
Cinnamon ground 1/4 teaspoon / 1g. (little) - hot - acrid, sweet .... *
Curd cheese 20% 5/8 lbs - 8oz / 250g. (little) - cool - sour........................ wood
Butter organic 2 teaspoons / 8g. (yes) - neutral - sweet............................. earth
Strawberry jam 4 table spoons / 50g. () - neutral - sweet, sour .... wood

Cooking instructions:

Preheat oven to 180°C/356°F.
Put Peaches briefly in boiling water, drain and peel off the skin. Cut
peaches into small slices.
Cook noodles in plenty of salted water until firm, drain, chill off cold and
drain.
Separate eggs. Stir egg yolks with icing sugar, vanilla sugar, grated
lemon zest and cinnamon until fluffy with the whisk. Stir in the curd

cheese. Add the noodles.

Beat the egg whites into firm snow and carefully lift them under the pasta.

Spread a baking dish thinly with butter. Alternating pate noodle mixture and peach slices into the form layers. Finish with the pasta mixture.

Sprinkle the casserole with butter flakes and bake in a preheated oven for 3o minutes.

Serve portion by portion with a tablespoon of jam.

9.22 Oat Congee

Forces Qi, forces liver and spleen, mcisturizes intestines, eliminates mucus, holds back sweat.

Cooking time approx. 2-4 hours

Calories p. portion: 162

3 portions

Allergens: A

Quantity of ingredients

Oat 1 cup / 125g. (little) - warm - sweet.. metal
Water 6 cups / 700g. (yes) - cool - salty ....earth

Cooking instructions:

Cook oats and water in a ratio of about 1: 6. The amount of water determines the thickness of the mash (pure matter of taste). The oats swell, so do not take much. Put the oats in a saucepan with good insulation and a heavy lid. It is important to simmer the oats after a short boil on the slightest flame, otherwise it burns. Cook the oat for 2-4 hours. The longer it cooks, the more he strengthens.

9.23 Polenta with peach

Strengthens blood and fluids, brings blood into motion, builds up Qi, spreads, strengthens stomach Qi, diuretic, moisturizes, relaxes, builds up Qi, spreads, warms the stomach and spleen, promotes blood circulation and conduction flow, relieves cold-sick

Cooking time approx. 20 min

Calories p. portion: 197

3 portions

Quantity of ingredients

Water 1 1/2 cups / 240g. (yes) - cool - salty .... earth
Corn Grease (Polenta) 1 cup / 120g. (rec.) - neutral - sweet .... earth
Peaches 2-3 pieces / 400g. (yes) - warm - sour, sweet .... earth
Vanilla pod 1 pinch / 1g. () - neutral - sweet .... *
Chili (pod or ground) 1 pinch / 0,1g. (little) - hot - acrid .... metal
Cinnamon ground 1 pinch / 1g. (little) - hot - acrid, sweet .... *

Cooking instructions:

Pour the polenta into a pan of hot water with constant stirring until the polenta has the desired consistency. Pull the polenta from the fire and let it soak for 10 minutes.

Wash fresh peaches and cut into quarters. Pour into the finished polenta the peaches, add the vanilla and add Chili to taste, stir and let it go for 3 minutes.

Winter varieties: Pickled fruit, pear, apples

9.24 Potato-basil soup

Strengthens stomach Qi, moisturizes, relaxes, builds up Qi, spreads, forces Qi, forces spleen, relieves inflammation, spreads, strengthens spleen and liver, regulates Qi flow.
Cooking time approx. 25 min
Calories p. portion: 96
4 portions
Allergens: L

Quantity of ingredients

Water 2 cups / 450g. (yes) - cool - salty .... earth
Potato 4 pieces / 200g. (yes) - neutral - sweet .... earth
Carrot 2 pieces / 100g. (rec.) - neutral - sweet .... earth
Celery root 1 piece / 500g. (yes) - cool - sweet .... earth
Pepper (ground) 1 pinch / 0,5g. () - warm - acrid .... metal
Ground 1 pinch / 1g. (rec.) - warm - acrid .... metal
Garlic 1 clove / 3g. () - hot - acrid .... metal
Salt 1 pinch / 1g. (little) - cold - salty .... water
Lemon 1 teaspoon / 3g. () - cold - sour .... wood
Basil (fresh) 1 Bunch / 50g. (yes) - warm - acrid, bitter .... metal
Sugar cane sugar 1 pinch / 1g. (little) - cool - sweet .... earth
Olive oil 1 table spoon / 10g. (little) - cool - sweet .... earth

Cooking instructions:
Peeled and chopped 4 medium potatoes in a pot of hot water and 2 chopped medium carrots, a piece of celery root, a pinch of pepper, a pinch of ground cumin, crushed a small clove of garlic, a pinch of salt, 1 teaspoon of lemon juice, simmer until the Vegetables is soft.

Add 1 bunch finely chopped basil into one half of the soup and puree everything; stir in the other half of the basil; with rose paprika, a pinch of whole cane sugar, 1 tablespoon of olive oil or butter, freshly ground pepper, salt to taste.

9.25 Pumpkin soup

Forces lungs and spleen, diuretic, forces Qi, protects liver, forces Qi, forces spleen, relieves inflammation, moisturizes, relaxes, builds up Qi, spreads, strengthens spleen and liver, regulates Qi flow, moisturizes, relaxes, builds up Qi, spreads.
Cooking time approx. 1 hour
Calories p. portion: 105
3 portions

Quantity of ingredients
Pumpkin 3/4 lbs / 300g. (rec.) - warm - sweet...earth
Carrot 2 pieces / 100g. (rec.) - neutral - sweet..earth
Potato 2 pieces / 120g. (yes) - neutral - sweet...earth
Olive oil 1 table spoon / 10g. (little) - cool - sweet.......................................earth
Onion white 1 piece / 50g. (little) - warm - acrid .... metal
Water 1 cup / 120g. (yes) - cool - salty..earth
Parsley 1 table spoon / 7g. (yes) - warm - bitter.. wood
Anise (Common Fennel) 1 pinch / 1g. (rec.) - warm - acrid.........................earth
Salt 1 pinch / 1g. (little) - cold - salty .... water

Cooking instructions:
Add the olive oil to the pan, add the diced pumpkin, diced carrots and potatoes. Roast them shortly, add the finely chopped onion, fill with water, add enough water to cover the vegetables at least 3 finger-widths. Boil at low heat.

Season with sea salt, add small cutted parsley, a pinch of anise (little). Allow to simmer for about 35 minutes. Then purée the soup and add some water, depending on the consistency of the soup.

9.26 Rice congee with carrots and fennel

Nutritious builds up Qi, forces the digestive functions.
Cooking time approx. 2 hours and more
Calories p. portion: 131
3 portions
Allergens: G

Quantity of ingredients
Basic recipe for a rice soup (Congee) 2 cup / 500g. (rec.) - neutral - sweet..... *
Carrot 2 pieces / 100g. (rec.) - neutral - sweet...earth
Fennel 1 piece / 250g. (rec.) - warm - sweet, little acrid..............................earth
Butter organic 1 teaspoon / 3g. (yes) - neutral - sweet...............................earth
Cardamom 1/2 teaspoon / 1g. () - warm - acrid... *

Cooking instructions:
Cook rice congee according to basic recipe.
Clean and cut carrots and fennel.

When carrots and fennel are cooked from the beginning, they serve
wholesomeness. If added shortly before the end of the cooking time,
taste and vitamins are retained.

Refine with butter and cardamom before serving.

9.27 Rice congee with honey pear and black sesame

Especially good in kidney Yin deficiency, moisturizes lungs, cools heat,
reduces lung mucus, produces humors, moisturizes, relaxes, builds up
Qi, spreads, moisturizes intestines, nourishes Yin.
Cooking time approx. 10 min - 3 hours
Calories p. portion: 158
2 portions
Allergens: N

Quantity of ingredients
Basic recipe for a rice soup 1 1/2 cups / 240g. (rec.) - neutral - sweet............. *
Pear 2 pieces / 300g. (little) - cool - sweet, sour ....earth

Cooking instructions:
Cook rice congee according to basic recipe.
Fill pot with 3 cm of water and heat till it boils. Quarter the pears (with
the skin and seeds) and simmer them covered with black sesame for 10
minutes. Mix with the rice.

9.28 Rice with parsnips

Regulates Qi, dries out, passes downwardly, warms the stomach and spleen, harmonizes the intestine, forces Qi, reduces moisture.
moisturizes, relaxes, builds up Qi, spreads. distributes mucus, activates Wei Qi, forces Qi.
Cooking time approx. 45 min
Calories p. portion: 206
3 portions

Quantity of ingredients

Rice variety any 1 cup / 120g. () - warm - sweet... .... metal
Water 1 1/2 cups / 200g. (yes) - cool - salty......... ....earth
Salt 1 pinch / 1g. (little) - cold - salty ....water
Parsnip 3-4 pieces / 450g. (rec.) - cool - bitter ....fire
Olive oil 1 table spoon / 10g. (little) - cool - sweet. ....earth
Sage 1 teaspoon / 3g. (little) - neutral - bitter, spicy ....fire

Cooking instructions:

Peel the parsnips and cut into slices. Fry for a short time in oil. Add the rice and fry again for a short time. Add the water and cook it at least 30 min. Sprinkle with fresh chopped sage.

9.29 Roasted millet with Celery sticks

Strengthens spleen and kidney, diuretic, brings the liver Qi in motion, cools heat, moisturizes, relaxes, builds up Qi, spreads.
Cooking time approx. 30 min
Calories p. portion: 400
2 portions
Allergens: L

Quantity of ingredients

Millet 1 cup / 120g. (little) - cool - sweet, salty...............................earth
Water 1 1/2 cups / 240g. (yes) - cool - salty..earth
Celery sticks 2 rods / 50g. (rec.) - cool - sweet ....earth
Water 2 table spoons / 30g. (yes) - cool - salty ....earth
Salt 1 pinch / 1g. (little) - cold - salty ....water
Sage 3-4 leaves / 2g. (little) - neutral - bitter, spicy ....fire
Cress 1 teaspoon / 3g. (little) - cool - sweet...metal

Cooking instructions:

Roast millet briefly, pour over water, heat till it boils and let stand for 20 min. to swell.

Cut celery into small pieces and mix with water, salt and fresh herbs and cook for 10 min. Add to the millet. Sprinkle fresh sage or watercress over it.

9.30 Rosemary Potatoes

Forces Qi, forces spleen, relieves inflammation, relaxes, builds up Qi, spreads.
Cooking time approx. 30 min
Calories p. portion: 188
2 portions

Quantity of ingredients

Potato 6-8 pieces / 420g. (yes) - neutral - sweet..earth
Olive oil 1 table spoon / 10g. (little) - cool - sweet ....earth
Rosemary 1 teaspoon / 2g. (yes) - warm - bitter ....fire

Cooking instructions:

Cut the potatoes into half´s, apply a little olive oil on the cut surface, then salt, sprinkle 2 - 3 rosemary needles on the potatoes.
Place the potatoes on the baking tray and bake them in the preheated oven for approx. 25 minutes to 190°C/374°F.

9.31 Semolina soup with vegetables

Strengthens spleen and liver, regulates Qi flow, relaxes, builds up Qi, spreads, dries out, passes downwardly, strengthens stomach Qi, strengthens spleen and liver, regulates Qi flow, moisturizes, relaxes, builds up Qi, spreads.
Cooking time approx. 20 min
Calories p. portion: 105
3 portions
Allergens: AGL

Quantity of ingredients

Basic recipe for a vegetable soup (nutritious) 2 cup / 500g. () - neutral - *.......*
Wheat semolina 2 table spoons / 20g. (yes) - cool - sweet, salty.............. wood
Lovage 1/2 teaspoon / 2g. (yes) - warm - acrid, bitter .... metal
Basil (fresh) 1/2 teaspoon / 1g. (yes) - warm - acrid, bitter........................ metal
Basil (fresh) 1/2 teaspoon / 1g. (yes) - warm - acrid, bitter........................ metal

Nutmeg 1 pinch / 0,1g. () - warm - acrid... .... metal
Carrot 1/4 lbs - 4oz / 100g. (rec.) - neutral - sweet.................................earth
Celery root 1/8 lbs - 2oz / 50g. (yes) - cool - sweet ....earth
Cream, sweet 30% 3 table spoons / 30g. (little) - neutral - sweet ....earth
Parsley 1 table spoon / 10g. (yes) - warm - bitter.................................... wood

Cooking instructions:
Roast wheat grits without fat in a pan. Roast the chopped carrots and celery briefly. Add the vegetable soup (Basic recipe for a vegetable soup). Season with lovage, nutmeg and let it 10 min. simmer.
Stir in the cream before serving and garnish with parsley.

9.32 Soup with egg yolk

Forces Qi and Yang, is very warming.
Cooking time approx. 5 min
Calories p. portion: 173
1 portions
Allergens: CO

Quantity of ingredients
Basic recipe for a beef soup (warming) 1 cup / 250g. () - warm - * .... *
Chicken yolk 1 piece / 25g. () - neutral - sweet ....earth

Cooking instructions:
Warm the beef soup according to the basic recipe for a beef broth, warm it up and jell the yolk.

9.33 Sugar pea soup with prawns

Strengthens spleen and liver, regulates Qi flow, strengthens the middle, diuretic, harmonizes Qi (in the middle and lower heater), forces kidney-Qi und -Yang
Cooking time approx. 15 min
Calories p. portion: 215
3 portions
Allergens: BL

Quantity of ingredients

Peas 5/8 lbs - 8oz / 250g. (yes) - neutral - sweet, salty..............................water
Basic recipe for a vegetable soup (nutritious) 2 cup / 500g. () - neutral - *....... *
Olive oil 1 teaspoon / 3g. (little) - cool - sweet...earth
Onion (spring onion) 1 piece / 20g. (little) - warm - acrid...........................metal
Parsley 1 Bunch / 15g. (yes) - warm - bitter .... wood
Olive oil 1 teaspoon / 3g. (little) - cool - sweet...earth
Shrimp 8 pieces / 120g. () - warm - salty... water
Salt 1 pinch / 0,5g. (little) - cold - salty .... water
Pepper (ground) 1 pinch / 0,1g. () - warm - acrid .... metal

Cooking instructions:

Cook the peas in a saucepan with water until soft, strain and quench with cold water. Mince the parsley, add to the peas and pour in the vegetable broth. Chop onions and fry in a little olive oil, add to soup and puree. Sauté the prawns in olive oil, cut into bite-sized pieces and add to the soup. Season with salt and pepper.

9.34 Tea from celery sticks

Brings the Liver Qi in motion, cools heat, moisturizes, relaxes, builds up Qi, spreads.
Cooking time approx. 15 min
Calories p. portion: 1
4 portions
Allergens: L

Quantity of ingredients

Celery sticks 2 table spoons (chopped) / 18g. (rec.) - cool - sweet............earth
Water 2 cup / 500g. (yes) - cool - salty..earth

Cooking instructions:

Heat the water till it boils and put it aside. Add cutted celery and cook for 10 min. to let go. Strain. Sweet to taste with honey.

9.35 Tea from ginger with honey

Strengthens middle heater, moisturizes, gets Qi moving, forces fluids production, reduces cold-evil, directs upwards.
Cooking time approx. 30 min
Calories p. portion: 5
4 portions

Quantity of ingredients

Ginger fresh 1 teaspoon / 3g. (rec.) - warm - acrid....................................metal
Water 2 cup / 500g. (yes) - cool - salty...earth
Honey 2 teaspoons / 6g. () - cold - sweet..earth

Cooking instructions:

Heat the water till it boils and put it aside. Add ginger and 20-30 min. to let go. Sweet to taste with honey.

9.36 Tea from peppermint with white sugar

Cools heat, distributes mucus, derives wind-cold and wind-heat, brings the stomach Qi in motion, solves congestion, forces Qi, moisturizes lungs.
Cooking time approx. 15 min
Calories p. portion: 8
2 portions

Quantity of ingredients

Peppermint 1 table spoon / 7g. () - cool - acrid, bitter ....metal
Water 2 cup / 500g. (yes) - cool - salty...earth
Sugar candy white 1 teaspoon / 3g. (little) - neutral - sweet.......................earth

Cooking instructions:

Heat the water till it boils and put it aside. Add peppermint and 10 min. to let go. Strain. Sweet to taste with honey.

9.37 Tea from thyme

Converts mucus, forces lungs and spleen, dr es out, passes downwardly.
Cooking time approx. 10 min
Calories p. portion: 0
4 portions

Quantity of ingredients

Thyme 3 table spoons / 6g. (rec.) - warm - bitter...*
Water 2 cup water / 500g. (yes) - cool - salty ....earth

Cooking instructions:

Heat the water till it boils and put it aside. Add thyme and 10 min. to let go. Strain. Sweet to taste with honey.
Drink 2 to 3 cups daily by mouth

9.38 Tea Green tea

Reduces internal heat, dissolves mucus, detoxifies.
Cooking time approx. 10 min
Calories p. portion: 2
1 portions

Quantity of ingredients
Green tea 1 teaspoon / 2g. () - cool - sweet, bitter ....fire
Water 1 cup / 120g. (yes) - cool - salty..earth

Cooking instructions:
For each cup you use a teaspoonful or a teabag.
Pour green tea only with 60 to 80 ° C / 140 to 176 °F hot water,
otherwise it will be bitter.
If the tea has a stimulating effect, let it draw for two to three minutes. It
has a calming effect for a duration of five minutes (no longer, otherwise
it will be bitter!).
Another method: Pour the tea leaves with about 70 ° C / 158 °F hot
water and pour the water immediately again. Then just pour hot water
again. The bitter substances disappear and the tea gets a milder
aroma.

9.39 Tea mixture against general exhaustion

Cooking time approx. 10 min
Calories p. portion: 2
4 portions

Quantity of ingredients
Lemon Balm (dried) 2 teaspoons / 3g. () - cool - sour .... metal
Blackberry leaves 2 teaspoons / 3g. () - neutral - bitter..................................... *
Lavender blossoms 1 teaspoon / 2g. () - warm - acrid, bitter .... *
Water 1 1/2 cups / 500g. (yes) - cool - salty..earth

Cooking instructions:
Heat the water till it boils and put it aside. Add 2 g lemon balm, 2 g
blackberry leaves, 1,5g lavender flowers, leave to stand covered for 10
minutes, then strain. Drink a cup three times a day.

9.40 Vegetable bowl with tofu and curry on rice

Cooking time approx. 30 min
Calories p. portion: 162
6 portions
Allergens: E

Quantity of ingredients

Olive oil 2 table spoons / 20g. (little) - cool - sweet ....earth
Garlic 2 cloves / 3g. () - hot - acrid .... metal
Onion white 1 piece / 60g. (little) - warm - acrid .... metal
Curry 2 table spoons / 16g. () - warm - acrid .... metal
Water 2 cup / 500g. (yes) - cool - salty..earth
Turnips 2 pieces / 50g. (rec.) - cool - bitter...earth
Pumpkin 1 piece / 400g. (rec.) - warm - sweet...earth
Carrot 1 piece / 100g. (rec.) - neutral - sweet..earth
Parsnip 1 piece / 150g. (rec.) - cool - bitter ....fire
Potato 1 piece / 70g. (yes) - neutral - sweet...earth
Sweet potato 1 piece / 70g. (rec.) - warm - sweet ....earth
Cauliflower 1/4 piece / 250g. (little) - cool - sweet ....earth
Broccoli 1/2 piece / 250g. (little) - cool - sweet...earth
Okra 12 pieces / 200g. (yes) - hot - bitter...earth
Soy Tofu 1 piece / 250g. (rec.) - cool - sweet...earth
Basil 3 table spoons / 12g. (yes) - warm - acrid, bitter ....fire
Salt 1 pinch / 0,5g. (little) - cold - salty .... water

Cooking instructions:

Heat the oil at medium temperature in a large, heavy casserole, add the garlic and onion and sauté with constant stirring. Sprinkle curry powder over it, fry gently for about 5 minutes and make sure that the garlic and curry do not
 burn. Add the water and heat till it boils. Gradually peel all vegetables, dice and add, starting with the varieties that
 need the longest cooking time. Once the water has boiled again,
reduce the heat and simmer the vegetables for about 15 minutes. When it is almost soft. Add the cauliflower and broccoli florets and the okra and cook the stew for another 10 to 15 minutes. Add the tofu during the last 5 minutes.

Cook the brown rice at the same time Sprinkle the rice in a medium saucepan with water, salt and cover for about 20 minutes. cook on a low heat. Take from the fire and another 10 min. to let go.

Arrange the stew over the brown rice and sprinkle with basil.

9.41 Vegetable potato and meat mash

Strengthens spleen and liver, regulates Qi flow, moisturizes, relaxes, builds up Qi.
Cooking time approx. 30 min
Calories p. portion: 127
2 portions

Quantity of ingredients
Potato 1/4 lbs - 4oz / 100g. (yes) - neutral - sweet....................................earth
Carrot (Early Carrot) 5/8 oz / 200g. (rec.) - neutral - sweet.........................earth
Beef meat (calf) 1/8 lbs - 2oz / 40g. () - neutral - sweet..............................earth
Apricots juice 6 table spoons / 60g. () - warm - sweet................................earth
Rapeseed oil 1 table spoon / 6g. (yes) - neutral - sweet ....earth

Cooking instructions:
Remove the flesh, skin, tendons and grease, wash under cool water and cut into small pieces and boil in a little water. After about 15-20 minutes, remove and puree. Wash the vegetables and potatoes, peel and cut into not too small pieces. Cook gently with a little water over a low heat for 10-20 minutes. Use the blender to chop the vegetables. Mix everything, add butter or oil and fruit juice and puree again.

Alternately use other meats such as chicken, lamb or turkey. Also change vegetables with zucchini, kohlrabi, fennel, pumpkin, parsnips and broccoli.

Also change the fruit juices. This can produce a variety of flavors.

9.42 Vegetable semolina soup

Strengthens spleen and liver, regulates Qi flow, builds up Qi, dries out, passes downwardly, reduces moisture, regulates Qi.
Cooking time approx. 20 min
Calories p. portion: 199
3 portions
Allergens: AEGL

Quantity of ingredients
Basic recipe for a vegetable soup (nutritious) 2 cup / 500g. () - neutral - *....... *
Potato 1 piece / 80g. (yes) - neutral - sweet...earth
Parsnip 1 piece / 180g. (rec.) - cool - bitter ....fire
Carrot 1 piece / 120g. (rec.) - neutral - sweet...earth
Celery root 3/8 lbs - 6oz / 150g. (yes) - cool - sweet ....earth
Kohlrabi 1/2 piece / 200g. (yes) - neutral - acrid, sweet ....earth

Beans (green, fresh) 1/4 lbs / 100g. () - neutral - sweet .... water
Wheat semolina 2 table spoons / 24g. (yes) - cool - sweet, salty .... wood
Lovage 1/2 teaspoon / 2g. (yes) - warm - acrid, bitter .... metal
Butter organic 1 table spoon / 20g. (yes) - neutral - sweet .... earth
Soy sauce 1 teaspoon / 3g. () - cold - salty .... water

Cooking instructions:

Worm the prepared vegetable soup; cook the vegetables in the soup softly. Spread some wheatgrass and let it swell. At the end, add lovage-green and a little butter and taste with soy sauce.

10 Effects of food

10.1 Use ingredients: recommendable

Anise (Common Fennel)
Basic recipe for a fish soup
Basic recipe for a rice soup (Congee)
Black caraway
Carrot
Carrot (Early Carrot)
Carrot juice without sugar
Celery sticks
Chicory
Coriander
Corn Grease (Polenta)
Endive salad
Fennel
Fennel tea
Ginger fresh
Gourd
Grapefruit (Pomelo)
Grapefruit dried peel
Grapefruit juice
Ground

Ground caraway
Lamb's lettuce
Leaf salads (bitter)
Lettuce
Miso
Oat flakes (whole grain)
Oat fusion (baby food)
Parsley root
Parsrip
Pumpkin
Radicchio
Rice Basmati
Soy Tofu
Spelled semolina
Sweet potato
Thyme
Turnips
Umeboshi plums (Japanese apricots)
Vanilla

10.2 Use ingredients: yes

Amaranth
Apricots
Arrowroot
Basil
Basil (fresh)
Black tea
Black-eyed peas
Boxhorn clover seeds
Butter organic
Carp
Celery root

Chervil
Chestnuts
Chicken egg
Clove
Coconut flakes
Cod
Couscous
Cumin (Caraway seed)
Dates dried
Dill
Fig

Fig dried
Fish pieces mixed (fresh water)
French beans
Goose
Goose parts
Grass carp
Hawthorn
Hazelnuts
Herbs various
Hyssop
Juniper berry
Kohlrabi
Kumquats
Lentils
Lentils black
Lentils red
Lentils yellow
Lovage
Marjoram
Mediterranean fish (cod, plaice,
haddock, sea eel, mackerel)
Morel (black, dried)
Mustard seeds
Oat flour
Octopus
Okra
Oregano dried
Papaya
Parsley
Peaches
Peaches (canned)
Peanut oil
Peas
Peppers

Peppers (rose peppers)
Perch
Pheasant
Pine nuts
Pistachios
Plaice
Poppy
Potato
Pumpkin seed oil
Pumpkin seeds
Quinoa
Radish black
Rapeseed oil
Rose hip tea
Rosemary
Sake
Salmon
Savory
Sesame paste (Tahini)
Sour milk cheese 20%
Soybean oil
Soybeans, black
Soybeans, yellow
Spiny lobsters
Star anise
Sunflower seeds
Turmeric (yellow root)
Vanilla powder
Walnuts
Water
Water hot
Wheat semolina
Wheat semolina for children

10.3 Use ingredients: little

Adzuki beans
Apple (sour)
Apple (sweet)
Apple juice (natural cloudy)
Apricot
Artichoke
Aubergine
Balm
Barley
Beer (Pils)
Beer (Top-fermented German dark
beer)
Bitter melon
Breadcrumbs (wheat bread, bread roll)
Broccoli
Brussels sprouts
Buckwheat

Bulgur (cereals)
Buttermilk
Calamari
Cashews
Cauliflower
Cereal coffee
Chard
Cherry
Cherry juice
Chicken meat
Chickpeas
Chili (pod or ground)
Chinese cabbage
Chives
Cinnamon ground
Cinnamon sticks
Clementines

Cocoa
Coconut grated
Coconut milk
Coffee
Coix (seeds) YiYi Ren
Cow's milk (1.5% fat)
Cow's milk (whole milk 3.5% fat)
Cream, sweet 30%
Cress
Curcuma
Curd cheese 20%
Curd cheese 40%
Deer meat
Deer meat
Duck (heart)
Duck (slaughtered)
Elderberry blossom tee
Feta cheese
Fresh cheese
Ginger powder
Goat
Goat and sheep's milk
Goat cheese
Grapes red
Lamb bones
Lamb meat
Leek
Lemon peel
Longane
Lychee
Lychee in Preserved
Margarine
Margarine (diet)
Millet
Millet flakes
Mozzarella
Multi-grain bread (gray bread)
Oat
Olive oil
Olives
Onion (shallot)
Onion (spring onion)
Onion read
Onion white

Oysters
Parmesan
Peanuts
Pear
Pear juice
Peas, green
Pepper white (ground)
Pomegranate
Pork skin
Quail
Quail egg
Quince
Rabbit meat
Raisins
Red cabbage
Rice (fragrance)
Rye
Rye flour
Sage
Salsify
Salt
Savoy cabbage / kale
Sesame oil
Soybean milk
Spelled (Dark) bread
Spelled grain
Spelled wholemeal flour
Spinach
Sugar brown
Sugar candy white
Sugar cane sugar
Sugar fructose - fruit sugar
Sugar glucose - grapes sugar
Sugar Milk Sugar
Sunflower oil
Tarragon (Estragon)
Turkey breast meat
Vegetable juice
Wheat flour
Wheat germ oil
White bread (wheat bread)
White cabbage
Wild boar meat
Zucchini

10.4 Do not use contra-acting foods

Agar agar (kelp)
Asparagus (green or white)
Avocado
Bamboo shoots
Banana
Banana (cooking banana)
Boletus mushroom

Burdock root tea
Carambola (Star fruit)
Champignon
Chanterelle
Crab
Cranberry
Cranberry juice

Cucumber
Currant (black)
Currant (red)
Currant (white)
Curry
Dandelionroots tea
Garlic
Gooseberry
Kefir
Kiwi
Lemon
Lemon juice
Lime
Mallow (Malva sylvestris) blossom tea
Mango
Mineral water
Miso paste (soy bean paste)
Mold cheese
Morel, dried
Mulberry fruit
Mullet
Mussels
Mutton
Nutmeg
Orange
Orange juice
Oyster mushroom
Pepper Cayenne
Peppercorns
Pickle
Pimento
Pineapple
Pineapple (from a can)
Pineapple juice without sugar
Plum
Pork meat
Rabbit liver
Radish
Radish (white, green, purple-red)
Reishi mushroom
Rhubarb
Sauerkraut (cutted cabbage fermented)
Seacrab
Shiitake, dried
Sorrel
Sour cherries
Sour cream 15% fat
Sour milk
Soy sauce
Spirit
Strawberries
Strawberry Juice
Sugar white
Tangerine
Tomato
Vinegar (Apple vinegar)
Vinegar (Red wine vinegar)
Vinegar Aceto Balsamico
Watermelon
Wild strawberries
Yarrow tea
Yogi tea
Yogurt (natural, 1.5% fat)
Yogurt (natural, 3.5% fat)

11 Complementary

11.1 Peppermint

Menthae, Herba
Preparation: Healing tea (infusion)
Relieves the internal wind of the body, clears the head and eyes, detoxifies the skin. Moves and regulates qi, lowering stomach-qi. Clarifying wind-heat, detoxifying, moving.
Pour 2-10 g with 250 ml of boiling water and let stand for 10 minutes. Then sieve. Drink 2 to 3 cups per day as needed.
Active ingredients: essential oil (menthol), tannins, flavonoids, bitter substances
Do not cook for long; Do not use on: Biao-Xu sweating or pregnancy.

11.2 St. Benedict's thistle, blessed thistle, holy thistle

Centaurea benedicta
Preparation: Healing tea (infusion)
Strengthens and regulates stomach-Qi and intestinal Qi, transforms mucus and moisture, and conducts, clears toxic heat, lowers fever.
The Benedictine herb has a certain allergy potential. The oil of the plant, which was used in purulent skin ulcers, acts bacteriostatic especially against staphylococci.

12 Basics of Nutrition

The basic principles of nutrition described herein are general recommendations. They are not aimed at a specific form of therapy. Recommendations concerning a therapy have priority.

12.1 Nutrition

Regular meals in a relaxed atmosphere. A warm breakfast is considered a good start into the day.
The main meals ought to be taken for lunch – supper in the early evening. Pay attention to feeling hungry or sated: don't eat too much nor remain hungry is the rule
Prepare the meals freshly from natural, regional products. Frozen, heat-conserved, industrially prepared or foodstuffs cooked in the microwave oven are rejected.
Choice of foodstuffs according to the season: more cooling food in summer, more warming food in winter.
Eat cooked food at least twice a day. Food and drinks ought to be lukewarm, never ice-cold or hot.
Raw vegetables, briefly cooked vegetables, freshly squeezed juices and mineral water are not recommended. Milk and dairy products are only included in the diet if they don't cause problems. Don't use therapeutic recipes over a longer period without consulting your doctor or therapist.

Varied food
Enjoy the diversity of foodstuffs. Characteristics of a balanced nutrition are variety, suitable combination and a balanced quantity of rich and low energy foodstuffs (on one hand avoiding undersupply with essential nutrients and on the other hand to take to many undesirable substances).

A lot of Cereal Products - and Potatoes

Bread, pasta, rice, cereal flakes (best wholemeal) as well as potatoes contain almost no fat, but many vitamins, mineral nutrients, trace elements, roughage and secondary plant substances. These foodstuffs ought to be taken with low-fat side dishes.

Vegetables and Fruit – „Take Five" every day ... 5 portions of

vegetables and fruit a day, as fresh as possible, briefly cooked, or maybe one portion as a juice – ideal as a side dish to every meal as well as snack between meals: Thus a lot of vitamins, mineral nutrients as well as roughage and secondary plant substances

Daily milk and dairy products

Milk and Dairy Products every Day, once or twice per Week Fish; meat, sausages as well as eggs moderately. These foodstuffs contain valuable nutrients like calcium in the milk, iodine selenium and omega-3 fat acids in saltwater fish. Meat is favorable due to its high content of disposable iron and the vitamins B1, B6 and B12. Quantities of 300 – 600 g meat and sausage per week are sufficient. Prefer low-fat products, especially in meat- and dairy products.

Low-fat and fatty Foodstuffs

Fat supplies us with essential fat acids and fatty foodstuffs contain also fat-soluble vitamins. Fat is high in energy; therefore much fat in the food may cause overweight, possibly also cancer. Too many saturated fat acids may further a tendency for cardio-vascular diseases in the long term. Prefer vegetable oils and fats (e.g. rapeseed-, olive-, soya-oils and solid fats produced therefrom). Beware of invisible fat in meat- and dairy products, pastry and sweets as well as in fast-food and convenience foods. 70 – 90 g fat per day is sufficient.

Moderately Sugar and Salt

Take sugar and foods/drinks containing various kinds of sugar (e.g. glucose syrup) only occasionally. Use herbs and spices as well as a little salt creatively. Prefer salt containing iodine.

Plenty of Liquids

Water is absolutely essential. Drink 1-2 l liquids every day. Prefer water (with or without gas) and other low-calorie drinks. Alcoholic drinks should not be taken.

Tasty Dishes, carefully cooked

Cook the meals with as low temperatures and as short as possible, using little water and fat – this preserves the original taste, keeps the nutrients intact and prevents the production of harmful compounds.

Take time and enjoy the food
Take your Time and enjoy your Food
Eating consciously helps to eat right. The eye enjoys food, too. It's fun, invites to enjoy varied dishes and stimulates the feeling of satiety.

Watch your Weight and stay in Motion
A balanced diet and a lot of exercise and sport (30 – 60 min/day) are a healthy combination. The right weight furthers well-being and health.
Thermals, directional effectiveness, digestive power
There are various criteria for judging the effectiveness of herbs and foodstuffs.
The use of certain herbs and ingredients is based on observations of the effects on the body which these foodstuffs, herbs and spices show after having eaten them. The medical science has developed following system: Every ingredient or herb has a directional effectiveness. Furthermore, there are herbs which have a special effect on certain organs.
The basic condition for a healthy metabolism is to obtain sufficient energy from food and that the digestive process doesn't use too much energy.
An easily digestible meal makes content and sated, doesn't cause flatulence and fatigue after the meal. The perfect spices increase the healthiness of our meals. Very often, just small doses of herbs and spices will suffice. They are not used to make us sated, but to help our digestive organs to digest the food.

12.2 Recipes

The recipes list the ingredients to be used and the cooking instructions show how the dish is prepared. The list of ingredients shows the concerned quantities as well as the relevance for the therapy. If you find „less than mentioned", try to comply or find an alternative from the „list of recommended foodstuffs". Mostly it shall result just in a small change of taste when you simply avoid this ingredient.
Mild cooking methods: boiling, stewing, poaching, steaming
Strong cooking methods: barbecuing, roasting, frying, smoking
Balanced cooking methods: deep-frying, baking brick
Deep-freezing and warming in the microwave oven should be avoided (denaturalization).

12.3 Foodstuffs

Foodstuffs have an effect on body and soul like medicinal herbs, only a very much milder one. Dietary advice is mainly based on regional foodstuffs. The knowledge about the effects of each foodstuff and the knowledge, when which foodstuff shall be used, is based on the orthodoschool of medicine. Use ecologic-organic products, if possible. As everything should be cooked for a long time due to a better digestability and very rarely eaten raw, the food agrees with everyone.
The classification of the foodstuffs according to their effect on the body is the basis in order to achieve a harmonious status of health.
Dietary advisors do not recommend certain foodstuffs for everyone. The individual diet is tailor-made for the individual constitution.

Buy only fresh and ripe fruit and vegetables. You ought to leave unripe fruit and vegetables and such with brown spots and wilted leaves behind in the market. In this case take deep-frozen goods (never ready-to-serve dishes!). Fruit and vegetables are deep-frozen immediately after harvesting and often contain more vitamins and minerals than the goods from the vegetable shelf. Whereas conserved or tinned goods contain very much less biological substances. Also, salt, sugar and others are mostly added to the latter. Never leave the foodstuffs in the water after washing them to avoid that many vital substances get drowned. Clean salads, fruit and vegetables immediately before serving.

Please make sure of the hygienic processing of foodstuffs. Clean your salads, fruit and vegetables carefully. When cooking with meat, prepare all ingredients first and then process the meat products. Clean the worktop and tools very carefully. Wooden surfaces ought to be treated with a mild disinfectant regularly in order to reduce germination.
Store fruit and vegetables separately, if possible. Harvested fruit and vegetables are still alive and emit e.g. ethylene gas, which makes other products ripen and age faster. Keep meat and fish in the closed packaging or store them in the fridge in closed containers.

12.4 Herbs

There are some basic rules for storing medicinal herbs. On principle, herbs must be protected from direct sunlight, humidity and heat.

Containers for the storage of herbs may be glasses, ceramic jars and even plastic containers. However, plastic is a rather unsuitable material and should only be a short-term solution. In case of glass containers, use a dark material.

Medicinal herbs cannot be kept for any long period. The shelf life of herbs is limited. However, it can be prolonged with suitable storage. The place should be dark, rather cool and absolutely dry. A wooden medicine cabinet, placed not directly next to a source of heat, would be ideal. Never buy large quantities of herbs so as not to have to throw them away. Label the container with the name of the herb and the date of harvesting or processing.

13 Other dietic-books

The following syndromes of dietetics, TCM or for a therapy supplement for cancer are available.

Dietetics

E001. Nutrition of the infant - baby food
E002. Nutrition during lactation
E003. Nutrition in old age
E004. Nutrition of children and adolescents
E005. Nutrition of athletes
E006. Light weight
E007. Pregnancy
E008. Full food

Protein and electrolyte - kidneys
E009. (hemodialysis) dialysis treatment
E010. Acute renal failure
E011. Chronic renal insufficiency
E012. Nephrotic syndrome
E013. Kidney stones (nephrolithiasis)

Gastrointestinal tract - pancreas
E014. Acute pancreatitis (inflammation of the pancreas)
E015. Chronic pancreatitis (inflammation of the pancreas)

Gastrointestinal tract - small intestine and large intestine
E016. Acute obstipation (constipation)
E017. Chronic obstipation (constipation)
E018. Colon irritabile
E019. Diverticulitis
E020. Acquired lactose intolerance (lactose malabsorption)
E021. Fructose malabsorption
E022. Glutensensitive enteropathy (celiac disease)
E023. Colectomy
E024. Short Bowel Syndrome

Gastrointestinal tract - liver, gallbladder, bile ducts
E025. Acute and chronic hepatitis (inflammation of the liver)
E026. Cholelithiasis (bile stones)
E027. fatty liver
E028. cirrhosis

Gastrointestinal tract - Stomach and duodenal intestine
E029. Acute gastritis
E030. Chronic gastritis
E031. Stomach bleeding
E032. Ulcus ventriculi and duodenal ulcer
E033. Condition after gastric surgery

Gastrointestinal tract - oral cavity and esophagus
E034. Stomatitis
E035. Esophageal carcinoma (esophageal cancer)
E036. Refluosophagitis (heartburn)

Special diseases
E037. Phenylketonuria (PKU)
E038. Rheumatic joint diseases

Metabolism
E039. Obesity (overweight)
E040. Diabetes mellitus
E041. Eating disorders (underweight)

Fat metabolism
E042. Hypercholesterolaemia (increased cholesterol level)
E043. Hepatic Encephalopathy

Heart and circulation
E044. Arteriosclerosis (arterial calcification)
E045. Heart insufficiency
E046. Hypertension
E047. Hyperuricaemia and gout

Changed nutrient requirements
E048. In case of fever
E049. For malignant diseases
E050. After burns
E051. Radiation and chemotherapy

CANCER
E100. Pancreatic cancer
E101. Bladder cancer
E102. Blood cancer (leukemia)
E103. Breast cancer
E104. Colorectal cancer
E105. Gastric cancer
E106. Kidney cancer
E107. Esophageal cancer

TCM
E200. Bladder - moisture heat in the bladder
E201. Bladder - moisture and cold in the bladder
E202. Bladder - emptiness and cold in the bladder
E203. Large intestine - external cold affects the large intestine
E204. Large intestine - moisture heat in the large intestine
E205. Large intestine - heat blocks the intestine II acute
E206. Large intestine - dryness of the colon
E207. Large intestine - Yang deficiency (cold)
E208. Heart - Blood insufficiency
E209. Heart - Blood stagnation

E210. Heart - Fire
E211. Heart - Hot mucus clogs the heart pores
E212. Heart - Cold mucus clogs the heart pores
E213. Heart - Qi deficiency
E214. Heart - Yang deficiency
E215. Heart - Yin deficiency
E216. Liver - Ascending Liver Yang
E217. Liver - Blood deficiency
E218. Liver - Blood stagnation
E219. Liver - Moisture heat in liver and gall bladder
E220. Liver - Fire
E221. Liver - Gall bladder Qi-Empty
E222. Liver - Cold in the liver meridian
E223. Liver - Qi stagnation
E224. Liver - Wind
E225. Liver - Wind with ascending liver Yang
E226. Liver - Wind with blood anemic
E227. Liver - Wind with extreme heat
E228. Lung - Qi deficiency
E229. Lung - Mucus-moisture in the lungs
E230. Lung - Mucus-heat in the lungs
E231. Lung - Mucus-cold in the lungs
E232. Lung - Dryness of the lungs
E233. Lung - Wind-heat attacks the lungs
E234. Lung - Wind-cold affects the lungs
E235. Lung - Yin deficiency
E236. Stomach - Bloodstagnation
E237. Stomach - Fire
E238. Stomach - Cold with liquid
E239. Stomach - Nutrition stagnation
E240. Stomach - Qi deficiency
E241. Stomach - Rebellious Qi
E242. Stomach - Yin Emptiness
E243. Spleen - Heat and moisture attack the spleen
E244. Spleen - Coldness and moisture affects the spleen
E245. Spleen - Qi deficiency
E246. Spleen - Qi deficiency + Declining spleen Qi
E247. Spleen - Qi deficiency + spleen does not control the blood
E248. Spleen - Yang deficiency
E249. Kidney - Heart and kidney no longer communicate
E250. Kidney - Jing deficiency
E251. Kidney - Kidneys cannot receive the Qi
E252. Kidney - Qi is not stable
E253. Kidney - Yang deficiency
E254. Kidney - Yin deficiency

For further information visit nutribook.info.

14 EBNS - Software for nutritional counseling

The main task of the database is to create personalized nutritional advice for each patient individually. The database was developed for Dietetics and Traditional Chinese Medicine.
The Database supports training and advices in the daily work routine.

The computer program provides lists of recipes, ingredients and herbs, which are given to the client. individually adjustable according to patient's request from whole food to vegetarians (lacto, ovo, ...). For every register there is an information sheet which can be given to the client. All texts can be individually designed.

The syndromes can be combined and result n an intersection of the recommended recipes and ingredients. The automated diagnosis for the TCM enables you to check your experience during the training as well as to confirm your diagnosis in the working day. You select several predefined symptoms and have the program automatically display the relevant syndromes.

How to work with the database:
Select the patient / client, select one cr more of the syndromes you diagnosed and print the folder.

You can change all values, create new symptoms or syndromes, develop recipes, change or adapt ingredients and herbs to your findings. In simple client management, all relevant data about the person is stored. You get an overview of the past diagnoses and the development of the course of the disease.
As a consultant you save a lot of time when you print out the recipe, food and herbal lists for the recognized syrdromes and give them to the clients. You can use this time for a personal conversation. With the database, dieticians and nutritionists can view the nutrients and trace elements for each recipe and develop recipes for syndromes even with suggested ingredients.
All recipe and grocery lists can also be ordered from me as a combination of several diseases. I wish all readers good luck, health and happiness in life.
More information can be found at www.ebns.at.
Volunteer: www.krebsinfo.at
Josef Miligui